Original title:
Fish in the Moonlight

Copyright © 2025 Creative Arts Management OÜ
All rights reserved.

Author: Clara Whitfield
ISBN HARDBACK: 978-1-80587-254-2
ISBN PAPERBACK: 978-1-80587-724-0

Celestial Currents of the Night

In the water, critters play,
Paddling under stars so gay.
They twirl and splash, a slippery dance,
Looking for a moonlit chance.

Bubbles rise in gleeful cheer,
As they wiggle, full of beer.
Laughter echoes from the shore,
As they plot a party galore.

Luminous Swimmers in Dreamy Depths

Glimmers spark in liquid lanes,
Giddy gills, and silly strains.
They flip and flounder, no cares to keep,
In their watery world, they leap.

With their pals, they spin and bend,
In underwater mayhem, they pretend.
A fishy prank, a splashy jest,
Who knew the night could be so blessed?

Reflections of the Night's Embrace

Shadows dancing, quite the sight,
Water sparkles, glowing bright.
A wriggly crowd, a boisterous show,
With each splash, they steal the flow.

Twists and turns, they act so bold,
While the moon smiles, watching the gold.
With fins a-flap and wriggles wide,
They toss their worries to the tide.

Aquatic Dancers Under a Silver Veil

Swirling motions, fins on spree,
Jigging joy, what glee to see!
A wobbly waltz in seaweed's embrace,
Two flippers tango, finding their place.

Playful pokes and nudges abound,
As they frolic without a sound.
With a flip, a spin, they seem to boast,
The quirkiest dance party, a fishy toast!

The Night's Aquatic Reverie

Under the stars, they splash and twirl,
In underwater parties, they twist and whirl.
With seaweed hats, and bubbles galore,
They laugh in the waves, who could ask for more?

A crab in a tux, what a fancy sight,
Waltzing with a clam, it's pure delight.
The octopus juggles with jellyfish glee,
While seahorses giggle, 'Come dance with me!'

Luminous Depths of the Lunar Tide

A mermaid laughs, her scales all aglow,
As sardines play tag, putting on a show.
With a flick of a fin, they dart through the deep,
Causing such chaos, no chance for sleep!

Then comes a whale, wearing glasses so round,
Taking a selfie while twirling around.
His friends all around, what a goofy crew,
Making sure the bubbles fly in every hue!

Rippled Reflections of Night's Embrace

Count the stars, oh what a view,
As a flounder croons a tune so true.
He's joined by a shrimp, in a chorus so bright,
Singing their hearts out, oh what a night!

A squidding sensation, with dance moves galore,
Spinning and twirling, always wanting more.
The currents are jiving, the waves in a swing,
Each little critter gets ready to sing!

Mysterious Dances of the Ocean's Veil

Bubbles pop like confetti, a grand soirée,
An eel in a bowtie has come out to play.
He twirls with a starfish, under the moon's glow,
Creating a whirl, a spectacular show!

Jellyfish jiggle, in outfits so bright,
While dolphins backflip, what a stunning sight!
With laughter and giggles, the reef's all aglow,
In this oceanic fiesta, let merriment flow!

Silver Scales Beneath Stars

Underneath the moon's bright glare,
A fish wears shades without a care.
With sparkly scales like disco balls,
He twirls and spins in watery halls.

His friends all laugh, a fishy crew,
In underwater Suits of blue.
While jellybeans drift with the tide,
They party hard with glee and pride.

Glimmering Tides at Twilight

In twilight seas, the bubbles pop,
A clownfish juggles—what a flop!
He slips on seaweed, takes a dive,
And lands in krill, oh what a vibe!

Sea horses wear their tiny hats,
Dancing around with silly spats.
The tides are full of giggly sounds,
As all the critters whirl around.

Lunar Dance of the Underwater

A big balloon floats past the base,
A fish hops on with comical grace.
They bounce and glide through bubbles bright,
Making a splash in the soft moonlight.

The coral choir sings a tune,
As shrimp do cha-chas by the moon.
An octopus leads with flailing arms,
His dance just oozes such great charms.

Reflections in the Night Waters

Under the stars, a tale unfolds,
With guppies sharing secrets bold.
A crab in glasses reads the signs,
While turtles ponder about designs.

They giggle at the swirling stream,
And plan a plot—a crazy dream.
To jump and flip, their hearts ignite,
In the wavy whims of the night.

Moonlit Pathways of Glimmering Souls

The stars above twinkle like pranks,
As shadows dance in gliding ranks.
With silver beams and giggles bright,
The walkway sparkles with pure delight.

A jumping jester leaps and dives,
In tides of humor, laughter thrives.
They splash and sway, a comic spree,
The moon whispers secrets to the sea.

Floating in the Realm of Night

In the pool of dreams, we drift away,
Bubbles of laughter lead the play.
A tickle from the waves below,
Swirling around in a wobbly show.

The giggles echo through the trees,
Like playful whispers in the breeze.
Jokes made of stardust and foam,
In this wild watery dreamland, we roam.

The Lure of Liquid Luster

A wink from Neptune, a cheeky grin,
Invites us in for a splashy spin.
With a swish and a flick, they play hide and seek,
Glittering like fools, they peek and tweak.

Catch me if you can, they tease with glee,
Dancing like marionettes on the sea.
Each sparkle a jest, each ripple a wink,
In this luminous pool, we grin and blink.

Twilight Currents Across Shimmering Seas

Under the moon's mischievous eye,
The waters bubble, laughter is nigh.
Tickled by waves, the currents play,
As giggling bubbles drift away.

A jester fish dons a crown of rays,
He sings a tune that sways and sways.
His fin a baton, he leads the dance,
In this aquatic circus, we take our chance.

Lunar Beacons Guiding the Silent Swims

Underneath the glowing sphere,
Swimmers giggle without a fear.
Bubbles pop like jokes afloat,
Fins hustle fast, in silly gloat.

Moonlit rays make shadows dance,
In watery halls, they take their chance.
With silly swirls and flips galore,
They leap and spin, then beg for more.

Tails wave like flags of merry cheer,
Each wink reflects their laughter near.
A wacky show in rippled tunes,
Where every joke gets lost with moons.

When tides tickle and currents play,
They find their reason to frolic away.
And in their game of gleeful dive,
It's the lunar lights that keep them alive.

Secrets of the Deep in Ethereal Light

Beneath the beams, a comedy, oh wow,
Whispers bubble in the current's vow.
A clam jokes with a silent pout,
While sneaky shrimp dance all about.

Starry gems tease the playful tide,
As fish giggle, they can't hide.
With silly faces, they paddle near,
In aquatic cabaret, nothing to fear.

The seaweed sways like a funky band,
Bouncing laughter across the sand.
Bright eyes spark in whimsical delight,
As creatures joke in the soft moonlight.

Secrets bubble up, what a delight!
In this patch of magic, hilarity's bright.
They share their tales in flippered cheer,
A splashy saga worth a beer.

Soft Glows of Aquatic Enchantment

Glimmers wink in the tranquil stream,
Where every ripple births a dream.
A jellyfish floats in a silly flare,
As laughter trails through the salty air.

School of fish in vibrant hues,
Performing antics, the latest news.
With twirls and spins, they stomp and prance,
In a liquid ballroom, they take their chance.

Creatures laugh under bright beams,
Their humorous plot, the best of schemes.
With fins that flutter, they joke all night,
In soft glows, they share delight.

Dancing shadows, a whimsical sight,
Each little splash brings pure delight.
In the calm waters, the fun won't stop,
As quips and giggles make the waves pop.

Dreamlike Ripples in the Moon's Gaze

Beneath the moon's watchful stare,
Fish tell jokes without a care.
Giggling fins in watery spree,
Crafting laughter like a melody.

Waves shimmer with a mischievous grin,
Where every flip brings a story in.
Bubbles echo with humorous cheer,
Creating a show we all wish to hear.

From the coral, the fans all cheer,
As creatures swim by with no fear.
With silly faces and playful play,
They make the night a fun display.

In rippling dreams, the fun flows free,
With every splash, a jubilee.
Laughter dances 'neath sparkling skies,
In nature's comedy, joy never dies.

Secrets of the Celestial Swim

Under starlit skies they glide,
Bubbles popping, nothing to hide.
Whispers of fins in the night,
Doing fishy flips, what a sight!

With a wink and a splash, they tease,
Turning tides into laugh-filled ease.
Dancing waves tell tales of glee,
Mischief swims, oh what a spree!

Kicking up sand in a swirl,
Each one a sly, slippery girl.
They twirl and swirl with a grin,
In this splashy joke, who will win?

Light-hearted shenanigans happen,
In the calm, the giggles worsen.
A secret world beneath the gleam,
Hilarious tides, a joyful dream!

Shimmering Shadows in the Deep

Glimmers of laughter flicker bright,
In the depths where the shadows bite.
Sneaky critters, with tricks they play,
Hide and seek in a watery ballet.

Curly tails spin and twirl,
Each wave reveals a slippery whirl.
Bubbles burst with a hearty cheer,
Tricky taps echo through the sheer.

Bubble parties in the deep,
Where secrets hide, and sillies leap.
Silvery fins flash like stars,
Underwater fun in their cars!

Riding currents without a care,
Each swish full of playful flair.
In the dark, they jest and tease,
Whimsical wonders, if you please!

Nocturnal Ripples of the Sea

Ripples giggle in the tide,
As fishy friends take a joyride.
With winks and waves, they swirl about,
In the night, there's laughter, no doubt!

Joking around with shimmering scales,
Chasing their own wiggly trails.
Ticklish tugs from lively peers,
Echo giggles that fill the spheres.

Frolicking in pools of mirth,
Creating chuckles beneath the earth.
Each splash a playful little joke,
As stars above shimmer and poke.

Cranky crabs join in the fun,
While jellybeans dance, oh what a run!
In the depths where the laughter unfolds,
Mirth and mischief, a sight to behold!

Dreaming in the Soft Silver Glow

In the glow where giggles meet,
Fish dream of adventures, oh so sweet.
Gliding through a silky sheen,
With tales of laughter, smooth and keen.

Flip and flop, with grace they dart,
Each twist and turn, a work of art.
Silent chuckles in the current flow,
Mirthful whispers where they go.

Nightly parties, they convene,
Floating in a silvered sheen.
Witty banter in every jest,
In the waters where they rest.

As tides roll in with sleepy dreams,
Making waves of silly schemes.
With each ripple, a playful shout,
In this sparkly world, there's no doubt!

Secrets of the Moonlit Waters

In the water, giggles play,
As shadows dance and sway.
Tiny fins in a big parade,
Swim around in a masquerade.

Bubbles burst like jokes untold,
Winking eyes, both shy and bold.
The stars above giggle too,
As the night shares secrets new.

A turtle tells a fishy tale,
Of moonlit pranks that never fail.
With silvery scales and silly spins,
They tease each other with playful grins.

Floating lanterns wink so bright,
Who knew the night could feel this light?
With laughter echoing through the tide,
Together, they enjoy the ride.

Reflective Journeys of Silver Glimmers

Silver trails on a wiggly path,
Jokes above cause a splashy laugh.
Fins and tails twirl like a show,
In this watery circus, spirits glow.

A crab does a tap dance on the sand,
While octopuses form a band.
They strum on seaweed, the bubbles rise,
As the moon watches with sleepy eyes.

Little guppies tell tall tales,
Of adventures far beyond the gales.
In each ripple, stories play,
Making waves of laughter sway.

Silly shadows cast below,
As starfish join the floating show.
With every giggle, they glide and gleam,
Creatures at play in a silvery dream.

Twilight Secrets Beneath the Surface

Beneath the waves, a party swirls,
With jellyfish winking in twirls.
They spin and dip under the starlit glow,
While seahorses giggle in toe-to-toe.

A pufferfish puffs up with delight,
He's the jester of the moonlit night.
As the crabs join in with cheeky grins,
The fun below is where it begins.

Clownfish chuckle and play peek-a-boo,
While lobsters dance in their fancy shoes.
Each splash and giggle, a secret shared,
In the playful depths, none are spared.

Laughter bubbles up from the sand,
An underwater band forms hand in hand.
With a twist and a twirl, they celebrate,
Beneath the moon, they cultivate fate.

Lunar Reflections in a Deep Blue Dream

Under the stars, a mirthful sight,
Wacky fish in a playful plight.
A school of jokesters darts and dives,
Creating ripples in their lively jives.

A dolphin flips with a comedic twist,
In this sea of glee, you can't resist.
With kelp hats on, they waddle about,
Making the nighttime sing with shout.

Anemones sway like they're in sync,
While sleepy eels nod without a blink.
They swap silly tales wrapped in sea foam,
In this watery kingdom, they all call home.

As night deepens, the laughter swells,
In the deep blue, where joy dwells.
Glorious pranks and whimsical schemes,
In a lunar moment, they all chase dreams.

Mystical Waters Where Shadows Roam

Beneath the surface, splashes glee,
Where shadows wiggle, wild and free.
A fishy wiggle, a silly dance,
With wobbly fins, they twirl and prance.

In glittering bubbles, laughter soars,
As creatures chuckle, behind coral doors.
A jellyfish giggles, a crab cracks jokes,
Even the seaweed, in laughter, wakes.

Enigmatic Glow of the Deep Seas.

A glowing spectacle in hues so bright,
As creatures bumble 'neath the shimmering light.
A clam opens wide, with a wink and a smile,
While the sea cucumbers strut in style.

The octopus juggles pearls with flair,
While sea turtles glide without a care.
With secret whispers, the tides would tease,
In this merry ballet, all swim with ease.

Silver Shadows Beneath the Tide

In shimmering shrouds, the fish take flight,
With flips and flops, they steal the night.
A sardine sings, a clumsy tune,
While the dolphins dance under the moon.

Anemones laugh with a tickling sway,
As shrimp on stilts put on a play.
Underneath waves, where mischief resides,
Every fish knows where fun abides.

Glimmering Scales and Starry Waves

With scales that glimmer, vibrant and bright,
A school of silliness swims in delight.
A playful puffer, with cheeks all round,
Makes bubbles of laughter while spinning around.

The starfish sit back, with arms spread wide,
As the clownfish joke, like they're taking a ride.
In watery whispers, the antics unfold,
In this silly realm, where joy is retold.

Aquatic Luminescence Under the Stars

Bubbles rise like laughter, so light,
In a sea full of wishful delight.
Flipping fins and a winking eye,
Cedric the clownfish, just passing by.

Squid dance like they're at a fair,
Wiggling their limbs without a care.
Splashing about like they own the night,
Setting the shores aglow with delight.

The stars giggle above the deep,
While playful crabs make a silly leap.
Everyone's welcome to join the fun,
In a watery world where jokes are spun.

With every wave, the laughter flows,
As jellyfish play, putting on shows.
Glowing bright, the sea's a sight,
Who knew the ocean could be so right?

The Night's Gentle Caress on Silent Waters

Ripples tickle the surface fair,
While minnows prance without a care.
Octopi juggle with such finesse,
In the moonlit water, we all confess.

Starfish wink from sandy beds,
Making wishes with goofy heads.
They dream of dancing at the tide,
As the sea turtles chuckle deep inside.

Caught up in currents of silly glee,
A catfish whispers, 'Come swim with me!'
We'll have a ball 'neath the starlit sky,
Comets zooming while we all reply.

Laughter's a current, drifting so free,
Join the parade, won't you just see?
With every splash, a tickle, a tease,
Under the stars, let's swim with ease!

Floating Dreams in Shaded Waters

Drifting by with a splash and a wink,
Dolphins laugh, bring champagne to drink.
Each ripple a giggle that dances around,
While seaweed sways, in soft atolls found.

A clam shrugged off all of his shells,
To host a party in watery swells.
We're munching on pearls and telling tall tales,
As bubbles float up like gossiping sails.

The deep is a bar where the mackerel meet,
Trading old stories while wrapping their feet.
What a fine view from this rippling seat,
Where everything's funny, in shades oh-so-sweet!

When shadows play games, who takes the prize?
Pufferfish puffing, oh what a surprise!
Floating along, life's a whimsical race,
In the depths of the waves, with a grin on each face.

Whispers of Twilight Among Coral Grottoes

The coral reefs gossip, all aglow,
As shrimp do the tango, a low-flying show.
Each fin and scale sparkles with cheer,
As sea urchins chuckle, 'What's happening here?'

Bubble-blowing fish, oh so spry,
Making their rounds like clouds in the sky.
While eels give high-fives with sly little grins,
The party is wild as the night begins.

Anemones sway with a rhythm divine,
Dancing to beats of the ocean's own line.
With winked eyes, all the creatures partake,
In a festival where no one's a fake.

Where creatures of night meet and collide,
In silly endeavors, they take great pride.
With laughter and joy, they all gather near,
The funniest ocean, oh what a cheer!

Moonlit Dreams of Aquatic Grace

In water's glow, a wiggly dance,
A curious crab takes a chance.
He slips on kelp, what a sight,
Crabs can't dance, but oh, what a night!

A jellyfish floats by, all aglow,
Wobbling wildly, putting on a show.
With tentacles swaying, it tries to prance,
But trip on a shell? Oh, what a chance!

A fish in slippers, with scales adorned,
Twirls around, as disco's reborn.
The seaweed swings to a sea shanty beat,
While the starfish claps with its five happy feet!

And as the waves crash, laughter grows,
Even the otters join in with their foes.
In this dreamy realm where giggles abound,
Ocean fun is the best playground found!

Starlit Realms Beneath the Surface

Beneath the stars, a wriggly treat,
An octopus knocks with its funny feet.
Dressed in polka dots, oh so spry,
It trips on a seaweed, oh me, oh my!

A dolphin bursts forth, doing the twist,
Eating popcorn shrimp, it can't resist.
With echoes of laughter, it splashes around,
Even the seahorses join the sound!

A crab wearing glasses takes in the view,
Reading the tide pool news—who knew?
Verbal squabbles in the deep ocean night,
With guffaws and giggles, what joyful delight!

As bubbles float upwards, dreams now awake,
Every sea creature's a jokester, make no mistake!
In starlit realms where fun freely roams,
The sea is a place we can all call home!

Midnight Serenade of the Deep

In waters of night, the creatures unite,
A turtle croons songs, oh what a sight!
With a top hat and monocle, quite the charmer,
It strums on a clam shell, the night grows warmer!

Nearby, fish giggle, passing a joke,
One tries to tell it, but just makes it poke!
Swimming in circles, they snort and they splash,
Like bubbles of laughter, a bubbly bash!

The angelfish prances, a tutu so bright,
While sea cucumbers dream in the night.
Corals clap softly, an oceanic cheer,
As gummy worms wiggle, they dance with no fear!

A narwhal tiptoes, a horned ballet,
With each little twirl, it sways away.
The midnight serenade fills the deep blue,
Where laughter and joy in the waves ensue!

Shimmering Tales of the Night Sea

Under shimmering waves, mischief is ripe,
Goldfish juggling bubbles, what a type!
With glittery scales that dazzle and gleam,
They put on a show fit for a dream!

At the reef's edge, the clownfish all prance,
With colorful wigs, they flaunt their romance.
But one little fish falls head over tails,
He flops on a rock, the crowd wails and hails!

A school of sardines, a synchronized line,
Flashing silver scales, they shimmer and shine.
But one gets distracted, off with the flow,
Now it chases seaweed, away it does go!

In tales of the night, where laughter prevails,
Every creature shares whimsical tales.
With shimmering flashes and cheerful delight,
The night sea is alive, what a wonderful sight!

Mystic Trails Under the Night's Glow

Underneath the silver bright,
A fish danced left, then leapt in flight.
With silly fins and playful grins,
It splashed around, causing spins.

The stars above let out a cheer,
As fishies frolicked, full of cheer.
With each big wave, they tickled toes,
In the night's glow, anything goes!

A clownfish wore a tiny hat,
While others giggled, 'Look at that!'
They swirled around the glowing tide,
With chuckles rising, side by side.

In this place, where wonders play,
Humor swims in a funny way.
As laughter echoes under the beams,
The sea is filled with wacky dreams.

Moonbeams and the Silent Swim

Beneath the beams, the water twirls,
Silly fish do silly swirls.
With a wink and a silly dance,
They lure the moon, it's quite the chance.

A catfish wearing oversized shoes,
Tumbled and turned, refusing to lose.
He bumped a crab, who waved hello,
And joined the party, putting on a show.

The moonlight shimmers, fish take the stage,
With splashing laughter, an aquatic rage.
Wiggly tails and fins that flap,
Create a scene where humor will nap.

As giggles bubble, it's plain to see,
The night brings joy, oh what a spree!
In aquatic realms, where jokes abound,
A hilarious night is here to be found.

Deep Blue Whispers: A Night's Journey

In waters deep, where whispers glide,
A fish told tales of a wild ride.
With snickers and wiggles, it spun about,
While seaweed laughed, there was no doubt.

An octopus played a game of tag,
With a flatfish—oh, what a brag!
They twirled and spun beneath the waves,
Creating fun, oh how it saves!

The turtles joined, in slow-motion style,
Rolling round, wearing a grin and a smile.
One shouted out, 'This is pure fun!'
As moonlit pranks had only begun.

With every ripple, giggles surged,
In this realm where the silly emerged.
As night unfolded, a joy-filled spree,
Under the stars, it was wild and free.

Shining Elegance Beneath the Sky

A flashy trout donned a bowtie neat,
With swishing tails, they joined the beat.
Add a wink and a twirl, oh what a sight,
This underwater party felt just right.

Starfish giggled, they couldn't help it,
As eels performed a graceful skit.
Their fins were flapping, so full of flair,
Creating smiles, floating in the air.

As dancing bubbles lightened the mood,
Puffers puffed up, all in a crude.
Their quirky shapes got everyone chuckling,
As waves of laughter rolled in, bubbling.

Beneath the stars, where fun takes flight,
The ocean glistened with pure delight.
This gathering brought joy to the floor,
In a shining dance, they all wanted more.

Secrets of the Tidal Night

When the tide pulls a prank, oh what a sight,
Little swimmers wear shades in the night.
They plot and they plan, in gleeful delight,
Trying to catch a glowbug, a silly fight.

Moon whispers secrets to the waves that sway,
Crabs dance a jig, trying to steal the play.
Stars giggle above, in a slumbering way,
As the seaweed sways like it's got something to say.

Jellyfish giggle with a glimmering grin,
In underwater raves, they take it on chin.
Splashing and dashing, making quite the din,
Who knew the deep blue had such a wild spin?

Glistening finned friends in their glittering hues,
Sing silly songs, while dodging the blues.
They swap hats and tails, like they're all in crews,
In this tidal circus, there's always good news.

Radiant Swirls in Twilight's Pool

Beneath dreamy skies, the waves start to swirl,
With critters who twirl, giving shells a good whirl.
A shrimp with a hat, he's a fancy young girl,
While sea stars gossip, they're in quite a twirl.

Splash! A fish with a bow tie makes quite a show,
Sardines spin circles, and then off they go.
A flamingo floats by, with a sketchy glow,
Under the glimmers, everyone's in the know.

The grand old octopus conducts the fun,
With eight little limbs dancing, oh what a run!
They high-five the clams, while the barnacles shun,
In this watery world, everyone's number one.

When twilight falls soft, the bubbles take flight,
They giggle and sway, such a curious sight.
With laughter like waves, they drift off in night,
Oh, what jolly friends in the star-speckled light!

A Dance of Light on Liquid Canvas

Upon the slick waves, there's a shimmer so bright,
   Toothed grins abound, it's a comedy night.
  A dolphin in shades, with style just right,
   Scoots past the plankton, a marvelous sight.

  Bubbles like balloons floating up to say hi,
   Sea cucumbers bobbing, oh me, oh my!
  With winks and with quirks, as they zoom by,
   In this watery world, they give it a try.

    An eel in a tutu is striking a pose,
While anemones giggle—their petals like prose.
A hermit crab chirps with a flair that just glows,
   In this underwater ball, anything goes!

As laughter spills forth from the depths of the sea,
   Even the starfish join in, oh, can't you see?
With every strange twirl, they dance wild and free,
   Painting this canvas, pure joy's jubilee!

The Enchantment of Watery Silhouettes

In the stillness of night, shadows frolic and tease,
With winks and with nudges in the gentle sea breeze.
A pufferfish laughs, with a nose full of cheese,
As jellybeans wink, through the currants they squeeze.

Glimmers of mischief on scales that just shine,
Every fin that's a twinkle works hard to outshine.
They spin silly tales, no need for a line,
In the depths of the ocean, joy's intertwine.

Octopuses whisper their secrets so sly,
While clams wear their pearls, playing shy as they lie.
With giggles and ripples, they all flutter by,
Creatures of wonder beneath the night sky.

So let the tides roll with a chuckle and cheer,
For these watery silhouettes have nothing to fear.
In the embrace of the waves, we hold our joys near,
In the laughter of currents, the night's crystal clear.

Celestial Currents and Ocean Dreams

In waters bright, a splash and swirl,
A clam's odd dance, gives us a twirl.
The jellyfish giggles, not quite shy,
Waves hold secrets of a deep sea pie.

A turtle winks, wears quite a grin,
Playing tag, race to begin.
Lobsters with hats, on a splashing spree,
Under starlit skies, wild and free.

In the deep blue, bubbles rise,
They tickle the seaweed, what a surprise!
Octopus juggling, oh what a sight,
Under the shimmer of the gentle night.

So gather your friends, take a dive,
In this ocean dream, we come alive.
With laughter and joy, the tide will sing,
In our watery world, let the fun take wing.

Shadows Play Where the Sea Meets Sky

The shadows dance on the ocean's face,
A crab in a top hat finds his place.
Penguins in tuxedos, they shuffle and glide,
While seahorses giggle, they can't hide.

Silvery fish wear shoes of bright hue,
They swim with a swagger, 'Look at us, too!'
A starfish spins like a disco ball,
As laughter erupts in the coral hall.

The seaweed sways, oh what a show,
With fish parade marching, a lively row.
As moonbeams wink, the ocean sighs,
In this delightful space where joy flies.

So come take a peek where shadows sway,
With giggling creatures who just want to play.
In the depths of the sea, dreams spread their fins,
Embrace the laughter, let the fun begin!

Ethereal Waters Beneath the Moon's Caress

In waters that sparkle like fairy dust,
A dolphin flips, it's a must!
Sardines in sequins do a quick parade,
While sea cucumbers turn, they've got it made.

With bubbles that bob, they form a crowd,
A sea otter's giggle, oh so loud!
Gummy sharks grin, not what you think,
As they dance around, making us blink.

The crabs play tag in a choreographed show,
Clams in clown costumes steal the glow.
Nautilus trumpets, a horn of delight,
In these ethereal waters, laughter takes flight.

Under the stars, the ocean's a stage,
With critters performing, oh so sage.
Join in the fun, let your spirits race,
In our watery world, find your place!

Starlit Serenades of the Deep

In the deep, where the starlights twinkle,
A fish named Bubbles loves to clinkle.
His jokes are splashes, silly and bright,
As eels roll over in pure delight.

Seahorses strut in tiny ballet,
With sea angels laughing all the way.
A clam opens wide, sings out a tune,
Creating waves that dance 'neath the moon.

With currents swirling, the silliness grows,
Crabs with kazoo mouths, music flows.
Turtles in caps, they lead the march,
In this starry sea, they steal the arch.

So raise a fin, join the melody,
In the depths of laughter, be wild and free.
For as night unfolds, let your spirit soar,
In the starlit serenade, we want more!

Starlit Waters and Whispered Dreams

In the night, the bubbles pop,
As gleeful fish start to swap.
With twirls and spins, they dance around,
Creating joy without a sound.

A playful splash, a giddy trait,
They chase their tails while swapping fate.
The moonlight glimmers, a shimmering tease,
As they perform in perfect ease.

They giggle as they whirl and glide,
Underneath the winking tide.
With every leap, a new surprise,
Creating laughs beneath the skies.

Oh, the tales that bubbles tell,
Of splashy antics, oh so well.
In starlit waters, joy takes flight,
As silly fish sing through the night.

Elysian Waves Under the Celestial Sphere

Beneath the glow, a quirky crew,
Swirls and jives, in skies so blue.
With every flick of fins so bright,
They brighten dark with sheer delight.

A clownfish prances, oh so brave,
As jellyfish dance just like a wave.
In bubbles, laughter floats and flies,
As moonlit shimmer winks and sighs.

The seahorse twirls in sparkling gala,
While crabs do the cha-cha with sheer sala.
A party under waves' embrace,
With a splashy smile, they find their grace.

To swim with glee, their motto loud:
In joyous waters, they're quite proud.
A symphony of giggles, sweet and clear,
In these elysian waves, they cheer.

Wanderers of the Midnight Blue

In the deep, the jesters roam,
With silly hops, they call it home.
Bubbles burst in cosmic cheer,
As wanderers swim with giddy leer.

One fish wears a hat, quite absurd,
While another strums on a shell so nerd.
They serenade the tides and gleam,
With jokes so good, they make fish beam.

With winks and nudges, they play tag,
While crabs join in with a sassy brag.
Every splash is a laughter-filled thing,
As the fish unite and joyfully sing.

The stars above can't help but grin,
As midnight blue twirls once again.
With finned companions, they weave and twine,
In the watery depths, life's simply divine.

Fluid Harmony in Moonbeam Traces

In liquid silver, the laughter flows,
As quirky fish strike goofy poses.
With fins like ribbons, they swirl and play,
Creating art in the ocean ballet.

A dodgy dolphin joins the fun,
Performing flips like it's a run.
While minnows giggle, all aglow,
Chasing each other to and fro.

In this midnight spectacle so bright,
Jellyfish waltz in the moonlit sight.
They wrap around with a gentle grace,
While every fish dons a silly face.

Among the ripples of gleeful cheer,
The sea's a stage for all to hear.
Fluid harmony, a whimsical spree,
In shimmering depths, forever free.

Ephemeral Beauty of Beneath the Glass

In the stillness of the night,
Bubbling bubbles take to flight.
Slimy creatures dance with glee,
A wiggly waltz beneath the sea.

With a flick, they make a splash,
In moonlit pools, they all dash.
Giggling bubbles, playful jests,
A game of hide and seek, no rests.

Their scales shimmer like a dream,
In this watery, funny theme.
Leaping high, they crack a joke,
As tides dissolve and waters soak.

Oh what fun beneath the tide,
With laughter flowing, side by side.
A secret world that we can't see,
Where silliness reigns, wild and free.

Caresses of the Night's Gentle Tide

As waves lap softly on the shore,
Crabs dressed up like knights galore.
Beneath the stars, they strut and cape,
A crustacean dance, there's no escape.

The ocean giggles, tales unfold,
Of slippery friends, both brave and bold.
As tides embrace the sandy land,
Silly splashes, oh so unplanned.

With twinkling eyes they tell a tale,
Of tidal tricks that never fail.
A moonlit party, what a sight,
Where all things sea dance with delight.

The night invites a giggling spree,
With salty jokes and giddy glee.
In this embrace of waves so wide,
Fun and folly slip and slide.

Ethereal Silhouettes in Celestial Flow

Under the moon's mystical gaze,
Shadows shimmy in the waves.
A playful game of peak-a-boo,
Where every flip brings laughter too.

Sardines spin in a merry chase,
While turtles slow dance, just in place.
Glimmering stars rock to and fro,
In this sea where giggles flow.

The currents tease with gentle hands,
Whisking away in merry bands.
Fish friends chuckle, sharing a wink,
In the cosmic tide, they always blink.

Beneath the glow of starlit skies,
Tall tales of bubbles and fishy lies.
Join the frolic, let's not be shy,
For in this realm, the silliness flies.

Shimmering Depths of Nocturnal Magic

In depths where shadows lose their way,
A slippery spirit starts to play.
With a swish, a flick, and a glee,
Dancing through the night's decree.

Octopus pranks, oh what a sight!
Changing colors left and right.
Bubbles giggle, surfacing fun,
In this watery world, we both run.

Starfish wave from their rocky perches,
Jellyfish float with gentle lurches.
Together they jest and gleefully spin,
Celebrating the chaos that bubbles from within.

At dawn they'll fade, but for now they gleam,
A comical procession, like in a dream.
Under the dark, they blurt and bind,
In the shimmering depths, where joy unwinds.

The Stillness of Midnight Reflections

In the pond, a splash and twirl,
A frog thinks he can dance and swirl.
With a hop here and a jump there,
He finds himself caught in the air.

The moon grins down, a shining guide,
And he's flailing about, no place to hide.
He quacks and quips, a comet of green,
While the fish roll their eyes, a sight unseen.

The turtles just laugh, with shells so round,
At the crazy ballet and the splashes all around.
Silly antics under silver beams,
Who knew underwater could hold such schemes?

As the night wraps up, the show takes a bow,
Our froggy friend thinks he's a superstar now.
But little does he know, with a splash and a glee,
Tomorrow it's bait, and he'll sing a new plea.

Dance of the Serene Under the Stars

Under the gaze of twinkling lights,
Swimmers rehearse for aquatic nights.
A crab in a top hat, with a monocle too,
Waltzes on waves—what a humorous view!

Dancing with jellyfish, so free of care,
They sway to the rhythm, a whimsical affair.
But one tangled up in the seaweed so green,
Looks quite ridiculous, a sight unforeseen.

With a scoot and a scuttle, they all take a chance,
Flipping and flailing in an oceanic dance.
The octopus leads—arms wide, what a sight,
He accidentally grabs a starfish's light.

As laughter erupts in the banter and glow,
The fish all agree, it's quite the show.
When morning arrives to claim the night,
They'll be bandmates again, with hearts so light.

The Deep's Secret Glow

In the depths where the seaweed flows,
Lives a wizard with enormous toes.
With a flick and a splash, he casts his spell,
Making bubbles that giggle and swell.

Glowing creatures with bright, silly faces,
Form a conga line through the sunken places.
A clown fish leads, with a rainbow grin,
Wiggling and shaking, let the fun begin!

A puffer fish puffs, what a sight indeed,
As the others laugh, he takes the lead.
But wait, what's that? A ticklefish came,
Sparkling with joy and igniting the game.

Swaying and swirling under oceanic glow,
With giggles echoing where the currents flow.
Their secret a treasure, shared in delight,
A party in the deep—oh, what a night!

Pelagic Reveries in Lunar Light

In the cool of night, when waters hum,
A dolphin dreams of the beating drum.
Riding the waves like a frothy cheer,
He dances with fish, spreading good cheer.

With a flip and splash, the group gathers near,
Seaweed confetti, oh what a sphere!
Clams join the party, shells clinking with pride,
While a shrimp boasts he's the best dancer on the tide.

With waves providing the jolly beat,
They twirl and they whirl, no hint of defeat.
Every gloopy bubble sings back to the moon,
While critters below hum an echoing tune.

Under the sparkle of starlit embrace,
Our ocean friends dance at their own pace.
As laughter erupts, they cherish the sight,
Love and joy glow in the heart of the night.

A Midnight Waltz Under the Stars

In a dance where the sea's always bright,
Giddy fish prance in the soft silver light.
They twirl and they leap, oh what a delight,
With tiny top hats, they're quite the sight!

As waves catch the giggles that sparkle and shine,
The crabs join the rhythm, they think it's divine.
With partners all flailing, not one seems to mind,
Just jiving through tides, oh how they unwind!

The moon peeks down, has a chuckle or two,
While dolphins do backflips, say 'Look at us, too!'
A school of fish wiggle, they shimmy in line,
Under sparkling skies, a true party divine!

With laughter and bubbles, they twirl and they spin,
Creating a ruckus with scales of bright skin.
As night saunters on, let the revels begin,
For the ocean's alive with the joys they all bring!

Shining Dreams of the Abyss

In the deep blue, where the winkles do glow,
A jellyfish jiggles, with moves quite the show.
Their tentacles sway like they're putting on airs,
While bloated pufferfish pretend they have flares.

A grouper glides by, with a sparkle and grin,
Telling tales of the sea and how fish like to swim.
But the anglerfish smirks in a shadowy seat,
Saying, 'Come here, my friends, for a surprise treat!'

They gather around for a feast on the floor,
Where bubbles are popping, and laughter does soar.
As seaweed confetti flies high through the air,
The creatures unite, as if without care.

With lanterns so bright and a zany buffet,
They waltz in the dark till the break of the day.
The abyss now a dance floor, they shimmy and sway,
Creating a ruckus, in the most fishy way!

Night's Aquatic Whispers

Upon the waves, there's a whispering tune,
Where seahorses chatter beneath the bright moon.
They gossip and giggle, oh what a delight,
Making plans for the circus that's coming tonight.

With eels as the acrobats, flipping about,
And crabs doing cartwheels, there's laughter, no doubt.
Octopuses juggle, and snails run the race,
While starfish sit clapping, a smile on each face.

The squid paint the canvas of dark with pure glee,
Creating a spectacle, wild as can be.
The fish all unite, they spread joyous cheer,
As the night brings them magic, they hold oh so dear.

With bubbles of laughter that rise to the sky,
The ocean's a stage, with performers nearby.
In this whimsical world, sleep is set aside,
As the creatures make memories with fun as their guide!

Essence of the Night Sea

In the depths of the blue, where the stars splash and dance,
Little fish flicker and try their own prance.
With bubbles for music and currents to ride,
They slide in the moonbeams, no worries belied.

The lanternfish lures with a wink and a smile,
Chasing away shadows, they swim for a while.
While turtles compete in a slow-motion race,
The jellyfish glimmer with a true touch of grace.

As ripples giggle under the night's gleeful watch,
The dolphins arrive with their flips and a swatch.
They play tag with the crabs, who just pinch and retreat,
Each moment unfolds, oh, so perfectly sweet!

The sea becomes a playground, where laughter is king,
With the ocean as home, joy is the real thing.
As dawn starts to peek, they'll all shout hooray,
For the essence of night is just fun in the sway!

Enchanted Waves under a Midnight Sky

Bubbles rise with a happy pop,
As the sillies around me flop.
Tails wagging in dances grand,
Underneath the stars they stand.

Splashes giggle, water splatters,
Jokes made up in glimm'ring patters.
A crab tells tales of a fishy scout,
With every tale, a laugh, no doubt!

Moonbeams tickle the ocean floor,
While starfish jump, they'll never bore.
Caught in the flow, who could resist?
Each wave is a wink, impossible to miss!

Dolphins dive, and laughter sings,
Each flip and splash brings silly things.
Under the glow, we dance and cheer,
Creating memories, loud and clear.

Moonlit Journeys in the Blue Abyss

Waves of giggles roll and sway,
A shoal of friends in a playful way.
They dodge and weave with little care,
While squids make faces from their lair.

Crabs wear hats, it's quite the sight,
As octopuses plan a wild night.
They host a party, what a spree!
Beneath the waves, we're totally free.

They toss around seaweed confetti,
While jellyfish glow all shiny and ready.
With each brush of the tide, they beam,
Having fun like it's a silly dream!

Under the stars, antics unfold,
With tales of treasure, they brag and bold.
In this watery pub, where friends unite,
Laughter echoes in endless delight.

Aquatic Whispers of the Night Wind

From coral reefs, the whispers play,
A fishy prankster's grand ballet.
With every splash, the giggles flow,
As seaweed sways to the show below.

A conch shell sings a merry tune,
While flounders dance like a cartoon.
They swap their tales, both tall and small,
As laughter rises, we heed the call.

Winking waves in the twilight's glow,
Each swirl a jest, as currents row.
Skip like a stone, a wobbly flight,
Chasing bubbles in sheer delight!

Seabass tell tales, huddled tight,
Making jokes of the ocean's bite.
Under the watchful, grinning moon,
The deep sea chuckles, a jolly tune.

Illuminated Schools in the Dark

In the depths where the sea life plays,
Schools of thought fish out their days.
They swirl and twirl like a merry ball,
A radiant dance beneath the sprawl.

Sardines in a line, what a sight!
With antics that bring such sheer delight.
Bubbles rattle with silly tales,
As they skewer the night with their gales.

The anglerfish winks, what a tease,
While clever turtles crack up with ease.
Whimsical whispers in the midnight tide,
Where laughter and lightfulness collide.

Under the stars, the party starts,
With giddy flops and fluttering hearts.
In the shadows, joy swims near,
Laughing echoes, we hold so dear.

Ethereal Echoes of the Deep

In the water, shadows dance,
Giggling bubbles lead the prance,
Fish in hats, a jolly sight,
Flip-flopping under stars so bright.

They throw a party, oh what fun,
With tiny shoes, they start to run,
A conga line through kelp so tall,
Wobbling fish, they might just fall.

A clownfish jests, a coral cheers,
They toast to laughter, banish fears,
With jellybeans, their favorite treat,
A underwater joke can't be beat!

As the tide rolls in for the night,
These silly fish won't stop their flight,
With bubbles blown, and giggles shared,
In the ocean's depths, no one is scared.

Nocturnal Glances Beneath the Surface

As moonbeams twinkle on the waves,
Sardines wear suits, like little braves,
A gleeful dolphin sings a song,
To help the crowd sing right along.

Spinning tales of seaweed forts,
Squids play chess, in underwater courts,
An octopus jokes, with arms to spare,
Tickling friends, without a care.

Crabs in tuxedos, bow ties in tow,
Strut across sand, putting on a show,
With pincers raised, they dance and sway,
As laughter echoes, through the spray.

The night rolls on, with giggles abound,
As sea creatures waltz all around,
No secrets kept, just joy and glee,
In the depths where the funny fish be.

Sapphire Glows in Still Waters

In the shallows, a shimmer bright,
Wiggly tails spark with delight,
A goldfish spins, a tiny swirl,
While sea stars giggle, giving a twirl.

The catfish tells a silly joke,
And nearby sea turtles start to poke,
With bright blue shades and beachy hats,
They laugh so hard, they scare the rats.

Dances unfold beneath the tide,
As sea urchins gladly glide,
With clapping shells, they join the fun,
Making memories, one by one.

A fish parade drifts near the shore,
Bringing chuckles, and oh so much more,
Sapphire waters, filled with cheer,
In the night, laughter's all you hear.

Silent Whispers Between the Ripples

Whispers travel through the night,
As fish conspire with pure delight,
They swap legends of the sea,
Where clowns wear wigs in jubilee.

A puffer fish gives quite a puff,
While seahorses say, "that's enough!"
With winks and jests, they start to play,
In ripples where the sea horses sway.

Turtles crack up, they can't contain,
While eels slide in, to join the game,
With a splash and giggle, they all agree,
This is the best of company.

As the night drifts on with glee,
The ocean's laughter sets them free,
Beneath the stars, life's but a jest,
In watery realms, they're ever blessed.

Shadows of Serenity in Charmed Waters

In the water, things swim and sway,
With tiny bubbles leading the way.
A shiny scale catches a glimpse,
As giggles echo, the night starts to wimp.

A turtle hums a little tune,
While the stars dance, bright and soon.
A crab in a hat, quite out of place,
Wearing his shell like a smiley face.

The soft plop of a joyous splash,
Makes ripples in waves that dash.
With silver scales, they twirl and spin,
As laughter bubbles up from within.

Moonbeams twinkle on the waves,
Where fish act like playful knaves.
Each turn a laugh, every splash a cheer,
In these waters, joy is near.

Gliding Through a Night of Liquid Magic

Beneath the shimmer, a party brews,
With guppies in tuxedos and flippered shoes.
A clownfish cracks a joke with flair,
As the angelfish flips its pretty hair.

A catfish dances, belly so wide,
While a tiny minnow takes a ride.
With bubbles afloat, the giggles ignite,
In this water, we find pure delight.

A turtle drops a beat so slow,
As seahorses twist in a merry show.
Each wave breaks with a burst of glee,
And underwater, we all feel free.

With the moon casting spells and beams,
The night winks as it fills our dreams.
Silver fins flash in the liquid light,
In this joyous realm, we party all night.

Wading Through the Veil of Twilight

When shadows stretch and colors blend,
The water calls, where dreams transcend.
With a splash and a splash, frogs join the beat,
As the fish wear hats, oh, isn't it sweet?

In this watery dance, some twirl and glide,
While a pufferfish lifts its pride.
The sun dips low, and giggles abound,
As the sea creatures jive all around.

A shrimp tells tales of underwater lore,
While octopuses juggle with an ocean floor.
With joyous glee in every twist,
Even the seaweed sways in bliss.

Jellyfish glow, painting the scene,
As fishes boast in shades of green.
A moonlit bash, no worries tonight,
All under the stars, what a pure delight!

A Tapestry of Reflective Midnight

In the stillness of the midnight tide,
Creatures of the sea come out with pride.
A lone goldfish spins in delight,
As moonbeams sparkle, oh what a sight!

A sea cucumber wearing a tie,
Floats by with a hint of a sigh.
With a wink and a splash, the gang arrives,
As the laughter ripples, the magic thrives.

The fish parade with quirky flair,
While jellyfish twinkle, floating in air.
Every bubble bursts with a cheeky grin,
In this midnight ball, we all fit in.

Under the stars, the currents weave,
A tapestry of joy, too good to leave.
As waves lap gently, we dance and play,
In the mirror of night, we laugh all day.

The Dance of Twilight's Aquatic Spirits

In the glow of shimmering light,
Sardines wearing hats, oh what a sight!
They twirl and spin with joyful cheer,
While crabs breakdance with no hint of fear.

A guppy in a tux, all dressed to impress,
Waltzing with an octopus, what a mess!
Sea turtles laugh, it's quite the scene,
As jellyfish jiggle in a disco routine.

Clams start a conga, all in a row,
While flounders flop, giving quite a show!
The party's a riot, a splash of delight,
As sea creatures frolic 'til the dawn's first light.

So grab your snorkel and join the fun,
Under the waves, the joy's never done!
With glee and bubbles, let's host today,
A lunar ball under stars' soft ballet.

Celestial Beauty of the Ocean's Depth

Stars wink down at a quirky parade,
As dolphins juggle while the clams serenade.
A seal wears glasses, looking quite wise,
Giving advice that's a bit of a surprise.

The angelfish strut in sequins so bright,
Throwing confetti, what a delight!
With a splash and a giggle, they dive and flip,
Under the moonlight, the ocean's own trip.

Eels do a limbo, oh what a twist!
They wriggle and squirm, it's hard to resist.
A grouper's got moves that could bring down the house,
While starfish cheer him, quiet as a mouse.

Their beauty twinkles in the vast marine,
Where laughter echoes, pure and serene.
In this underwater rave, we lose all dread,
As the night turns fun in hues of red.

Nurtured by Night's Gentle Caress

Moonbeams dance on watery tracks,
As clownfish tell jokes to a pack of whacks.
A hermit crab's shell is a tropical stew,
Where the party starts early, at one and at two.

The tides are a giggle, rolling with glee,
As the seaweed waves like it's waving to me.
A shrimp on a trumpet spins tunes so loud,
Drawing a crowd from the bubbling crowd.

Mussels play cards, with a wink and a nudge,
While the octopus' plot seems a little dodgy.
In this funny realm, where the critters delight,
Each splash of laughter sails through the night.

So join in the revels, let your worries fade,
In the ocean's embrace, the fun won't evade.
Under starlit skies, we all interlace,
With smiles like bubbles, in this joyful space.

Beneath the Stars, Among the Waves

Beneath the stars, where the sea meets the ray,
Fish don their hats for this nautical play.
A pufferfish travels with pomp to spare,
While sea horses dance with a delicate flair.

With barnacles snickering, they join the fun,
As every sea critter races, it's never just one.
Seahorses jump rope with kelp for the twirl,
While the slippery eels do a twist and a whirl.

Anemone pranks from its sandy throne,
While squids throw ink like it's confetti blown.
With laughter a-splashing, the sea's in a spin,
As the night grows younger and the fun begins.

So let's share a wink with the moon, oh so bright,
As the currents carry delight into the night.
In this underwater circus, with each little quip,
We'll laugh with the tide, on this festive trip.

Beneath the Luminous Expanse

Beneath the stars, they wriggle and gleam,
Silly swimmers with a twisted dream.
Bubbles pop like giggles in glee,
A dance of fins, wild and free.

Moon's bright grin reflects on the tide,
Where laughter echoes, they cannot hide.
With wobbly turns, they do the cha-cha,
Their slippery tails say, "Oh, ha-ha!"

In this watery ballroom, they prance and sway,
Making rainbows as they play.
Glistening scales, a disco delight,
Under the shimmer of the night.

Twinkling orbs and giddy delight,
Who knew prey could dance with such might?
They flounce and frolic and flip with ease,
Oh, the joy found beneath the trees!

The Poetry of Night in Flowing Tides

Under bright stars, they twirl and tease,
Giggling bubbles ride the gentle breeze.
Glowing swirls in their silvery race,
With all the grandeur of an artful chase.

In silken waters, they play peek-a-boo,
Making waves giggle, who knew they could too?
A twist of a fin, a shimmer gleams,
Crafting laughter in the moonlit dreams.

A wobbly flip, a splashy ballet,
With cheeky grins as they glide away.
Beneath the stars, they gather in flocks,
Clocking their moves like aquatic clocks.

Full of mischief and merry disputes,
They spin and swirl in shiny new suits.
With every flip, a chuckle released,
Dancing with joy, never deemed least!

Murmurs of Waves Under a Velvet Sky

Ripples giggle where night meets the shore,
Singing tales of splashes and lore.
In moonbeam light, their antics unfold,
As shimmering stories are told.

With jiggly jumps, they steal the show,
Swimming in circles, oh what a flow!
Each flicker and flip, a prank in the air,
Making onlookers giggle with flair.

The gurgles and burbles take center stage,
A comedy script, one can't disengage.
In this watery circus, they tease the crowd,
With silly dances, they're feeling proud.

At night's encore, they bow with spunk,
Spinning in whirlpools, with joyful hunk.
With splashes of laughter, the waves do chime,
As nature's jesters perform in their prime!

Celestial Swirls Beneath Moonlit Skies

In a glow of silver, they glide with cheer,
Boisterous bubbles rock musicians near.
Splashing tunes with a flick of their tails,
Like comical pirates setting their sails.

With every twist, a goofy surprise,
Mirthful creatures with sparkling eyes.
Who knew the depths held such joy?
In antics reflective, it's never coy.

As twinklings wink from the skies above,
Wiggly warriors dance, full of love.
Each little fin, a jester's delight,
In this whimsical world, all feels right.

Stars chuckle down at the swirling show,
While companions cheer with a buoyant glow.
As mirth flows freely through every tide,
Under the night where secrets abide!

www.ingramcontent.com/pod-product-compliance
Lightning Source LLC
Chambersburg PA
CBHW060136230426
43661CB00003B/446